MW00653201

NAME: Candy Craig

DATE: January 7th
2017

This one is for you ♡

WERK 101

GET-YOUR-LIFE
TOGETHER
GUIDE

WRITTEN BY
KOEREYELLE

HEALTH, WEALTH, & LIFESTYLE LESSONS
FOR MODERN-DAY WOMEN

Werk 101: Get-Your-Life-Together Guide

Copyright © 2015, 2016 by Koereyelle DuBose

ISBN 978-0-9837182-5-3

Library of Congress Cataloging-in-Publication: 2016930740

Perfectly Imperfect Publishing Company

Printed in the United States of America

♡
THIS ONE
IS FOR YOU

Ready to get your life together once and for all? Well, look no more, you've picked up the right handbook. This book is dedicated to the modern-day woman who is dedicated to herself. She is a woman who wants more in life, sees a brighter future, and dares to dream big. She is a woman who is ready to stop wishing that her dreams will come true and start WERKing to achieve her goals, and live a life full of healthiness, wealthiness, and happiness.

INTRODUCTION

> **❝ Don't be the woman with the most to say and the least to offer. ❞**
>
> *- Koe*

YOU ARE A GAME-CHANGER. You are the one the world has been waiting for, and this guide was created with YOU in mind. Even past mistakes and bad occurrences can't stop a modern-day woman who is ready to *WERK* toward a more fulfilling, happier life. Get ready to let go of your old mentality and be liberated as I show you how to create a powerful, positive mindset, prepare for the man you've been praying for, and design your life's destiny on your own terms.

This book isn't meant to be read in one sitting. Instead I encourage you to *WERK* through it at your own pace, giving yourself time to digest and apply the newly found information. You'll find random lifestyle lessons, quick reference lists, journal activities (labeled as Let's *WERK!*), and plenty resources to **get-your-life-together** and take you one step closer to becoming the woman you're meant to be, a Queen — the one God created you to be.

Whether you "think" a lesson applies to your life or not, be open-minded and complete it. Then watch how an opportunity to use your new knowledge will present itself like magic.

These important steps will help make this handbook *WERK* for you:

- As you come to an affirmation, I challenge you to speak it aloud and really let it resonate in your spirit.
- Take your time going through the *WERK*sheets, lessons, and exercises. It's better to complete them thoroughly with a clear mind than to rush through them. Let them *WERK* for you! Be real with yourself

so that you truly can develop into the best version of yourself.

- Be patient with whom you are becoming. Don't try to recreate yourself overnight. Focus on one aspect at a time and make gradual improvements that will last a lifetime versus quick fixes that won't last two weeks.

- Develop your own "theories" based on the content of this book. Take what is useful, apply it to your life, and leave the rest behind.

- Don't rush out to share your new wisdom with all of your friends. Honestly, they may think you're crazy. If they do, it's not your fault. Everyone won't be ready to create a new mindset just because you are.

- As you read, make note of your "aha" moments. Feel free to write, underline, highlight, and mark in this book as needed. Make the most of it. Celebrate EVERY single accomplishment as you incorporate the lessons in your life. Every small change that you make or difference that you see in your life counts toward the big payoff. The more you celebrate, the more you'll have to celebrate.

Let's *WERK*!

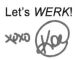

xoxo

THE **WERK** ING

woman's

WAY OF LIFE

MINDSET MANTRA

STRAIGHTEN YOUR CROWN & *embrace* your throne

BE YOUR OWN BOSS

The **statistics** don't DETERMINE success...keep your *eyes on the prize* 👁

PUT IN *WERK*

YOU ARE THE DESIGNER OF YOUR DESTINY

WATCH FOR THE SIGNS

▶ PURSUE YOUR PASSION WITH PATIENCE, PERSISTENCE & POSITIVITY

USE YOUR FAITH TO TURN OBSTACLES INTO OPPORTUNITIES

SAY YES when it *feels* GOOD

TRUST YOUR INTUITION

LET LOVE *lead* YOUR LIFE

FOLLOW YOUR ♡ AND GOD WILL DO HIS PART

YOU ARE *beautifully* & abundantly blessed

THERE IS NO COMPETITION

👉 WERK!

NOBODY CAN DO YOU LIKE YOU

You DON'T HAVE TO BEG BORROW OR SETTLE FOR ANYTHING

Prescriptions
NATURAL/HOMEOPATHIC
HEALTH & WELLNESS REMEDIES

Affirmations
POSITIVE PHRASES
THAT SHIFT YOUR MINDSET

Quotes
POWERFUL MESSAGES
THAT INSPIRE & EMPOWER YOU

Lifestyle Lessons
TIPS, TRICKS & TOOLS TO BUILD
YOUR PERSONAL BRAND, PURSUE
YOUR DREAMS & PUT YOURSELF FIRST

A GAME-CHANGER DOESN'T LIVE BY THE RULES. SHE *CREATES* HER OWN

You only have one life to live, and it is time to start living, not just existing, but really living. Wake up everyday excited about the possibilities because you are creating the life you want. Break the rules that no longer serve you. When you release the opinions of others and stop limiting your abilities, you can focus on what you want and what makes

A GAME - CHANGER DOESN'T LIVE BY THE RULES. SHE *CREATES* HER OWN

you happy. You're now in position to cut the ties that bind you and finally write your own liberating rules. Learn to trust your instinct enough to know what works for you and what "rules" you want to live by.

MIRACLES
& money
find me wherever I go.

2

CREATE A
WEEKLY
"TO-DO"
LIST

Spend
Sunday
night creating
a detailed plan
for the week. I
suggest adding the
most important events
to a time-management
app, such as Google
calendar (which syncs to your
phone). Your "To-Do" list will be
easily accessible and will keep
you focused and on schedule.

3

ADD AFFIRM-ATIONS TO YOUR "TO-DO" LIST

There's power in the spoken word. I started this trick, and the results are AMAZ-ING. Add statements such as "Expect a contract," or "New partner-ship proposal or a happy surprise," and watch how quickly they will appear in your life.

4

GO ON A TIME - MANAGEMENT DIET

Where did the time go? If you've ever found yourself saying this, then you know how valuable time is. Once your time is gone, you can never get it back. Prioritize your life to ensure that you're spending every moment wisely. Get in the habit of tracking your time to see if it is being well spent or if adjustments need to be made.

Make Room for
YOUR THOUGHTS

_____

_____

_____

_____

_____

_____

_____

_____

_____

_____

_____

_____

_____

_____

_____

_____

_____

5

MASTER THE "ONE-SONG" SHOWER

When I'm in a hurry, the One-Song Shower can be a lifesaver. I use it as my timer. When the song is over, my time is up.

My Notes: _____

_____

_____

_____

TURN YOUR PAIN INTO A PAY-CHECK

Long story short. In 2010, I ended an engagement that became a toxic and abusive situation. After my then-fiance's efforts to diminish my self-esteem failed, I spent the next eight months on a journey of self-discovery. I channeled my physical and invisible wounds and delved myself into self-help books. What started as a single woman's mission to

TURN YOUR PAIN INTO A PAY-CHECK

search for answers and seek self-improvement, evolved into an international women's empowerment movement called The Single Wives Club™. Everything truly happens for a reason and the most successful entrepreneurs are those whose profit began as a problem. They're the ones who have a lesson to teach the world based on their personal experiences.

TURN YOUR PAIN INTO A PAY-CHECK

Identify your pain. Take an honest assessment of the lessons learned

There has been something in your life that probably caused a tremendous amount of pain and taught you a major lesson. Figure out the underlying message and find a way to teach it to the world. Have you been a victim of domestic abuse? Did you

TURN YOUR PAIN INTO A PAY- CHECK

manage to lose a tremendous amount of weight for whatever reason? Have you mastered interviewing skills because of your stint with unemployment? If so, you've been given a special lesson to teach the world.

It was there all along
My lesson: I realized that I was unpre-

TURN YOUR PAIN INTO A PAY-CHECK

pared to become a wife because I had not fully become a woman. Through The Single Wives Club™, I'm now able to help thousands of single ladies become better women before becoming wives. Starting a member-ship-based organization with engaging workshops was easy. When I created a list of my gifts, talents, and skills, I realized that I've

TURN YOUR PAIN INTO A PAY-CHECK

always loved organizing people and planning events. For as long as I could remember, I've been organizing my friends, groups at school, events at work, etc. This is something I naturally do and love to do. I also discovered that part of my purpose is to educate and empower women. So, I've taken the training I received in obtaining my degrees along

TURN YOUR PAIN INTO A PAY-CHECK

with my experiences as an elementary school teacher to now create curriculums and plan lessons for the *WERK*shops I teach. Although I'm no longer a classroom teacher, the years dedicated to developing those skills were not lost, just redirected. Today, I'm receiving the payoff from the pain that I endured by organizing events for the purpose of

TURN YOUR PAIN INTO A PAY-CHECK

women empowerment and self-development.

My Notes: _____

_____

_____

_____

_____

_____

_____

" Ignorance is not bliss."

Whether you believe it or not, nature has a ton of vitamins and supplements that aid in optimal health. There are so many alternatives to prescriptions, copays, and "practicing" doctors. When my girl Jerri became a Master Herbalist, I asked her for a list of must-have vitamins and supplements. Below are five that she shared and that you should consider adding to your medicine cabinet. *Consider consulting your physician and/or do your research before taking any new supplements.*

Multivitamin. Multivitamins are essential to maintaining whole and complete health. However, whole food plant-based vitamins are preferred in this case. They are easy on the stomach and readily accepted by the body.

NATURAL/HOMEOPATHIC HEALTH & WELLNESS REMEDIES

One-A-Day vitamins may not provide the body with enough dosage or too much at one time.

Probiotics. Putting the good bacteria back into the colon is difficult when we are constantly exposed to toxins and chemically processed foods. A healthy gut leads to a healthy immune system. At least 10 billion organisms and 8 different strains of good bacteria are pivotal to choosing a probiotic.

Fish Oil. Omega 3,6, and 9 are key to maintaining youthful skin, moisturized hair, strong

Looks like it's time for a shopping trip!

joints, vision, and cardiovascular heart health. This supplement is often frowned upon due to the after-effects of smelly burping and its unpleasant taste. But good news. Supplements come flavored, and are now enteric-coated to prevent the fishy burping smell.

Grapefruit Seed Extract. Believe it or not, I found that this supplement works wonders for eczema. It is also used for high cholesterol, cancer, weight loss, and even fungal infections.

My Notes: _____

_____

Maca Root. Nicknamed "nature's viagra" increases stamina and enhances energy. Women typically use maca for hormone imbalance, menstrual problems, depression, stomach cancer, and so much more.

My Notes: _____

_____

_____

_____

_____

D.A.R.E. TO DREAM

Deter-
mine your
destination.

What do you
want? You are the
designer of your
destiny. To achieve your
goals, you have to be clear
and know where you're going.

Apply the lessons you've
learned.

It is not about what you know; it is about

7
CONTINUED

D.A.R.E. TO
DREAM

what you do. To bring your dreams to life you must apply all of your new knowledge. In other words, put in the *WERK*.

Refuel your faith frequently.

Faith comes by hearing. This may mean weekly church services, daily meditation and journaling, or hourly affirmations.

D.A.R.E. TO
DREAM

Educate yourself.

In order to live a life you love, you must become a lifelong learner. The more you know, the more you'll grow.

My Notes: _____

_____

_____

Life rewards me everyday, happy *surprises* are on the way.

8

SIX POSITIVE WAYS TO START YOUR DAY

Inspired by:
Diamonde Williamson,
Author

1. Laugh.
2. Visualize
   a beautiful
   day ahead.
3. Affirm yourself.
4. Read a few pages
   from an inspiring
   book.
5. Write a few sentences in
   your gratitude journal.
6. Speak a few words of thanks
   ALOUD to your Creator.

9

A SALAD A DAY KEEPS THE DOCTOR AWAY

One thing we commonly leave out of our diet is raw food. By eating a salad each day, we assist our bodies in breaking down the other foods we consume.

My Notes: _____

_____

_____

_____

10

YOU DON'T HAVE TO CHASE WHAT GOD SENT

What is meant for you is already yours. You will not be required to beg, borrow, or steal. Here's a simple rule to always remember: If you have to force it, it isn't for you.

My Notes: _____

_____

_____

_____

11

BE A CHAMELEON

Who will you be today? When I am hosting an event, I know that I must be friendly, outgoing, and helpful. When I am running a meeting, I know that I must be serious, firm, and knowledgeable. When I am out with my friends, I know I can be silly, wild, and fun. Be a chameleon, and let your environment dictate your character.

Most Common Crystals

Crystals have been used for healing the body, transforming the spirit, inspiring intuitive insight, guarding against negative vibrations, and smoothing the energy flows of spirit and body.

According to Ancient Feng Shui, the power of the crystal can be found in its structure – growing and reaching up toward light from the deepest parts of earth. It is a conductor of energy– both as a receiver and a transmitter. Your personal crystals will attune themselves to your vibrations, as you will attune to the natural vibrations of the crystal.

" Crystals have been used for healing the body..."

It is important to keep your crystal clean in order to protect it from outside negative vibrations. Certain colors are used in healing and magical manifestations with specific effects. For best results, choose crystals that speak to you or that you feel attracted to.

Red: Grace, purification, tolerance, patience, focus, acceptance, passion, healing guilt, blame, and anger.

Orange: Surrender, spiritual presence, valor, spontaneity, discrimination, happiness, joy, and enthusiasm.

Yellow: Gratitude, creativity, individuation, focus, inspiration, inventiveness, strength, courage, and individuality.

Green: Contentment, harmony, serenity, peace, balance, generosity, empathy, and temperance.

Blue: Charity, devotion, compassion, reciprocity, intelligence, humility, heart wisdom, and purity.

Indigo: Mercy, forgiveness, integration, wisdom, justice, intuition, synthesis, and structure.

" Your crystals will attune themselves to your vibrations..."

Violet: Joy, freedom, abundance, detachment, centeredness, fairness, responsive, fortunate, and inclusive.

White: Integration, wholeness, foundation, spontaneity, cycles of fertility, potential, clarity, receptivity, and directness.

My Notes: _____

_____

_____

_____

_____

"STOP LETTING

SMALL-MINDED

PEOPLE TELL

YOU THAT YOUR

DREAMS ARE

TOO BIG."

- KOE

12

DON'T FEED THE FEARS

There are two emotions from which many others originate: FAITH and FEAR. We can either have faith that things are always working in our favor, or we can surrender to fear. Today, I encourage you to let faith lead you toward the direction of your dreams. Expect the fears to surface, but be determined not to feed them with your attention. The next time

DON'T FEED THE FEARS

fear
knocks, let
faith answer
the door.

My Notes: _____

_____

_____

_____

_____

_____

_____

_____

I am *beautifully* and **ABUNDANTLY** blessed.

"NO" MEANS NOT YET

You are
guaranteed
to experience
more than a few
"no's" along your
journey. One thing
that you can guarantee
is that no one has the power to deny you anything
you truly desire, unless you
give them permission to. When
someone tells you "no," it doesn't
mean it can't be done. It simply
means it can't be done with them.
Each day is a new opportunity to turn

13 CONTINUED

"NO" MEANS NOT YET

those "no's" into "yeses."

My Notes: _____

_____

_____

_____

_____

_____

_____

_____

"GOD NEVER

LETS YOU TAKE

A LOSS.

CONSIDER IT A

LESSON LEARNED. "

- KOE

14

ASSETS VS. LIABILITIES

Self-awareness is everything, and it is better to be responsible for how you act before someone else has the opportunity to bring it to your attention. In an effort to save face, complete this quick exercise to reveal something new about yourself. It is my signature "selfie check" that will help increase your self-awareness.

15

GET YA MIND RIGHT

You can't create new experiences with an old mindset. Make an effort to read a new book each month and meditate daily. For free meditation resources visit www.meditation-oasis.com

My Notes: _____

_____

_____

Apple Cider Vinegar

Apple Cider Vinegar (ACV) is literally a miracle juice. It smells gross and tastes bad, but ACV is a lifesaver. There's nothing more versatile, natural, and affordable. Not only does it have major health benefits, it also has several household uses. Some people like to take a shot of ACV, but I prefer to mix 2 tablespoons in a bottle of water and drink it throughout the course of the day. My favorite brand is Bragg's, which can be found at almost every health food store and even your local grocery store. During an episode of Dr. Oz, he talked about a bunch of new uses for ACV, and after a quick Google search, a zillion more uses were revealed.

My Notes: _____

_____

Here are a few ways to use ACV:

For skin, teeth, and hair:
- Use as a hair rinse to fight dandruff and add body and shine
- Use as a facial cleanser to boost the pH balance of your skin
- Add to bath water to relieve the redness and pain of sunburn
- Reduces buildup on the scalp
- Helps in the removal of warts
- Reduces swelling and fades bruising
- Skin toner for blemishes
- Reduces cellulite
- Helps control bad breath
- Whitens teeth and kills mouth bacteria
- Use as an overnight soak to clean dentures

NATURAL/HOMEOPATHIC HEALTH & WELLNESS REMEDIES

For health:
- Use as a detox to cleanse the kidneys
- Drink or supplement to prevent flu
- Reduces inflammation from arthritis
- Relieves sinus pressure and fights infection
- Aids weight loss by decreasing appetite and increasing fat burn
- Relieves allergies and asthma symptoms
- Relieves gout
- Balances the body's pH level
- Lowers cholesterol
- Reduces blood glucose level in diabetics
- Removes nail fungus
- Soothes bug bites and other minor skin irritations
- Aids digestion
- Taken with warm water and honey before

bedtime, ACV may help with sleep issues
- Strengthens bones
- Has anti-inflammatory properties
- Relieves pain from jellyfish stings
- Aids in relieving chest congestion
- Promotes bowel movements and eases constipation
- Relieves heartburn
- Can help stop hiccups
- Promotes sinus drainage
- Treats ear infections
- Soothes rashes
- Helps control sugar cravings
- Helps cure strep throat

"...There's nothing more versatile, natural or affordable!" - on Apple Cider Vinegar

- Helps treat eczema
- Increases energy and boosts metabolism
- Relaxes sore muscles
- Disinfects wounds
- Boosts immunity
- Lowers blood pressure

For the home:
- Use as a natural disinfectant cleanser
- Use it to wash windows to leave a streak-free shine and clean scent
- ACV is a natural deodorizer
- Use it to deter cats from having accidents (they won't urinate where they smell vinegar).

My Notes: _____

_____

Make Room for
YOUR THOUGHTS

_____

_____

_____

_____

_____

_____

_____

_____

_____

_____

_____

_____

_____

_____

_____

_____

_____

_____

16

YOUR HEALTH IS YOUR WEALTH

Without your health, all other goals are unattainable. Make a conscious effort to take better care of yourself by tracking what you eat and how it makes you feel. Think outside of the prescription bottle by researching an alternative to a medical doctor. Most major cities have integrative health centers that offer more than just prescriptions. They combine Eastern and

YOUR HEALTH
IS YOUR
WEALTH

Western
medicine to
provide a
holistic
approach to health
and wellness. Some
great wellness practic-
es include: reflexology,
iridology (eye reading),
ionic foot detox, vaginal
steaming, and acupuncture.

Natural Healing

I once met a woman who had spent
$19,000 on fertility treatments. She later

YOUR HEALTH
IS YOUR
WEALTH

heard about acupuncture and got pregnant after three months of treatment. Then there's a woman who healed herself from fibroids with crystal healing therapy. I know these two women personally, so imagine how many other women around the world found success outside of the traditional doctor's office or hospital visits.

17

YOUR HAPPINESS IS IN YOUR HANDS

Not theirs, but yours. No one has the power to make you happy but you. When you put your happiness in someone else's hands, they will disappoint you every single time. It is literally impossible for someone to "make you happy." Your happiness depends on you alone.

Finding my purpose gave me that "in

17 CONTINUED

YOUR HAPPINESS IS IN YOUR HANDS

love" butter-fly-in-my-belly feeling that I'd been chasing in men for so long. It was truly priceless. I want to encourage you to dig deep to find the courage to be happy.

Here are five ways to own your happiness:
1. Stop telling the same old story, it is time to write a new one.

17 CONTINUED

YOUR HAPPINESS IS IN YOUR HANDS

2. Don't subject yourself to solitary confinement. Put value in developing relationships.

3. Balance it out. *WERK* hard; Play hard.

4. Enjoy the journey and appreciate the process.

5. Be patient with yourself.

18

PUT YOUR PRIDE ASIDE

Pride goes before a fall (Proverbs 16:18) Stop being too good to ask for help and too strong to be vulnerable. If you know you're going through something that is beating you up and on the verge of breaking you down, then get help. When you can't release negative thoughts out of your mind and find yourself replaying past failures over and over in

PUT YOUR
PRIDE
ASIDE

your
head, you
are literally
stopping
yourself from
enjoying life. You're
blocking your blessings
and sabotaging your
success. Stop putting
yourself in solitary confinement and get the assistance
you need. You owe it to yourself to
invest in both your mental and
emotional health. There are a million
coaches, therapists, and support groups

18 CONTINUED

PUT YOUR PRIDE ASIDE

in your area. Need a therapist? Here are two I highly recommend:

Nikhol B. Jackson,
Transformational Coach
Nikholbjackson@gmail.com

Shaneka McClarty,
Licensed Therapist
Smcclarty@therapygirl.net

All the money
I spend now
comes back
to me
multiplied.

PUT IN
WERK

You can WISH or you can *WERK*. Nobody is handing out success. You gotta go out and get it. Dedicate yourself to your dream by spending one full hour each day building your brand and *WERK*ing toward accomplishing your goal. Did you know that one hour is only 4% of your day? You owe yourself at least that. Use this time to research, write,

PUT IN
WERK

conduct
meetings,
send emails,
etc.

*Discipline yourself
for 30 days and
watch your business
grow.*

When I teach my *WERK*-
shops, I always tell my students
how important it is to invest in
themselves and their future. My
favorite phrase is "You can WISH or
you can *WERK*."

PUT IN
WERK

WERK is a term that I use to refer to the time and effort dedicated to your dream. It's the energy used to design your destiny. It's the time after working your corporate job that you spend building your personal brand. It's the commitment to reading books to enhance your craft. All these are what I call putting in *WERK*.

PUT IN
WERK

When
you're able
to find time
each day to
invest in yourself,
you will begin to see
major payoffs. You've
heard that anything worth
having is worth working for.
With all of the lessons you've
learned, you owe it to yourself
to live a life you love.

_____

_____

_____

_____

_____

_____

_____

_____

_____

_____

_____

_____

_____

_____

_____

ACT AS THOUGH YOU ALREADY ARE

You are who you say you are. One of my favorite *WERK*ing women Patrice C. Washington, The Wisdom & Wealth Money Maven spoke life into her brand by introducing herself as a bestselling author even before her book was complete. She literally spoke her position into existence. You are who you say you are even if people can't see it yet.

20

CONTINUED

ACT AS THOUGH YOU ALREADY ARE

Practice what you want to experience, and it is guaranteed to show up in your life.

My Notes: _____

_____

_____

_____

_____

_____

_____

NATURAL/HOMEOPATHIC HEALTH & WELLNESS REMEDIES

Are You Good to Go Down Below?

In reference to American women who uses tampons, the average amount totals about 16,800 in a lifetime, according to The Huffington Post. Keep in mind that I know that this is a highly debatable topic. But, have you ever stopped to consider how tampons affect your health? During a vaginal steam session, an herbal-infused detoxing treatment that targets the vaginal area, the Certified Womb Sauna Practitioner warned me about the dangers of tampons and pads. I love my lady parts, so I had to do a little research and what I found was startling. Here it goes:

- Tampons and pads contain pesticides.
- Most tampons sold in stores are chlorine-bleached and made 100% from rayon.

- Tampons and pads with odor neutralizers and other artificial fragrances are nothing short of a chemical soup laced with artificial colors, polyester, adhesives, polyethylene, polypropylene, and propylene glycol, contaminants linked to hormone disruption, cancer, birth defects, dryness, and infertility.
- Sanitary pads are subjected to the same considerations as tampons when it comes to the fibers and chemicals used to treat the fibers.

The bottom line? None of these chemicals should be anywhere near your body, let alone inside your body. But there is a cure. I would never list all of these jaw-dropping facts without giving you a solution. My favorite

alternative to toxic tampons are (all-natural)
herbal pads from Lhamo. These natural sanitary napkins are infused with five essential
oils: Lavender (anti-inflammatory); Rose (pain
relief); Mint (refreshing feeling); Aloe (moisturizing); and Houttuynia (antiviral). They create
a safer alternative to the chemical-filled commercial pads we have used for years.

To order a pack of herbal pads visit:

www.ivpure.com

" I love my lady parts so I had to do a little research…"

21

LEAVE IT AND
BELIEVE IT

Many times we over-think, worry, and doubt ourselves right out of our blessings. The toughest part is learning to trust the process. Once you've mastered that, the world is yours.

My Notes: _____

_____

_____

22

WHY WORRY? IT PROBABLY WON'T HAPPEN ANYWAY

Instead of being pessimistic and worrying about what could go wrong, focus your energy on the possibility of what could go right. Worrying doesn't add another second to your life. Begin each experience with a positive expectation, and you will achieve a positive outcome. When you find yourself concerned or full of anxiety, learn to let go and let God.

22 CONTINUED

WHY WORRY?
IT PROBABLY
WON'T
HAPPEN
ANYWAY

Everything
is unfolding
perfectly at the
perfect time.

My Notes: _____

_____

_____

_____

_____

_____

_____

_____

I create a
MASSIVE & PASSIVE
wealth.

23

REMAIN
UNBOTHERED

You may not be able to control your circumstances, but you're certainly in control of your responses to them. When life hits, straighten your crown and don't step down from your throne for anyone.

My Notes: _____

_____

_____

ACT LIKE A LADY:
8 WAYS TO
IMPROVE
YOUR
ETIQUETTE

1. Learn to listen with your mouth closed.

2. Always send thank you notes to show gratitude and appreciation.

3. Appropriately tip your waitress, valet, hairstylist, and any other service worker who is allowed to accept gratuity (10%-20%).

4. Turn your phone on silent and put it away during meetings and meals.

24
CONTINUED

ACT LIKE A LADY:
8 WAYS TO
IMPROVE
YOUR
ETIQUETTE

5. No business calls before 9 a.m. or after 9 p.m.

6. Save the gossip for your girlfriends. Don't get caught being catty in public.

7. Do NOT show up late for yoga or meditation class and try to sneak in quietly. It is an impossible task and it will annoy your teacher.

8. Facetime should be a personal, private conversation. The world doesn't

ACT LIKE A LADY:
8 WAYS TO
IMPROVE
YOUR
ETIQUETTE

need to
hear or see
your video
chat with your
boo. Keep those
conversations
private (this rule
applies to talking to bae
on speaker phone, too).

My Notes: _____

_____

_____

25

TRUST THE TIMING OF YOUR LIFE

The same God who made a way last time will make a way this time.

My Notes: _____

_____

_____

_____

_____

_____

_____

WOW THEM WITH THE 30 SECOND RULE

Inspired by John C. Maxwell, Author of "25 Ways to Win with People"

Within the first 30 seconds of a conversation, say something that leaves a lasting impression. This is a simple way to make an easy connection. People everywhere need encouragement, and it doesn't take much effort to make someone's day. Plus, we never forget the people who make us feel good. Remember these words from Dr. Maya Angelou, *"I've*

WOW THEM WITH THE 30 SECOND RULE

Inspired by:
John C. Maxwell, Author
of "25 Ways to Win
with People"

learned that people will forget what you said, people will forget what you did, but people will never forget how you made them feel."

My Notes: _____

_____

_____

27

SHARE YOUR
STORY

Each and
every one
of us has a
unique set of
experiences, an
interesting perspec-
tive, and an exciting
story to share. Even if
you're not interested in
becoming an author, there's
no reason you shouldn't start a
blog. Blogs are a great way to
share your thoughts and connect
with like-minded people who appreciate your perspective. *Plus, blogging can*

27 CONTINUED

SHARE YOUR
STORY

be an additional stream of income once you begin increasing your audience of influence.

My Notes: _____

_____

_____

"IT'S NOT ABOUT

WHAT YOU KNOW,

BUT WHAT

YOU DO. "

- KOE

28

TAME YOUR TONGUE

Inspired by:
Lakia Brandenburg,
The Wife Coach

The power of life and death lies within your words. Every word you speak creates your situation. Choose your thoughts, intentions, words, and actions carefully, and speak the life that you desire into existence.

My Notes: _____

_____

_____

29

SMILE. IT AWAKENS THE ANGELS

Awaken the angels in your life by greeting them with a genuine smile. A smile is the universal signal of happiness, and there's always someone watching you who has the power to bless you.

My Notes: _____

_____

_____

30

WHEN SOMETHING TELLS YOU, LISTEN

Have you ever said to yourself, "Something told me I shouldn't have ...", or "Something told me I didn't need to ...". When something tells you, LISTEN. Your intuition is a gift. It will never fail you if you learn to listen. The more you use your intuition and follow your instinct, the stronger it becomes. Go with your gut and learn to trust yourself.

CHECK YOUR
SURROUNDINGS

Take a
moment to
analyze all the
relationships
you're in (friend-
ships, family
relationships, business
partnerships, and
romantic relationships) and
figure out if you are gaining
as much as you are giving or if
you are taking more than you are
giving. Everyone in your life is either
an asset or a liability. It's up to you to
remove and release anyone who no

31 CONTINUED

CHECK YOUR
SURROUNDINGS

longer
adds value
or isn't moving
in the direction
of your dreams.

My Notes: _____

_____

_____

_____

_____

_____

_____

_____

ATTITUDE IS EVERYTHING

Your
attitude
determines
your altitude,
and a kind spirit
can take you places
all the skills in the
world can't get you to. Be
conscious of how you come
across and communicate.
Make every effort to be friendly
and welcoming.

My Notes: _____

_____

_____

33

ACT LIKE ROYALTY AND THEY'LL TREAT YOU LIKE A QUEEN

People learn how to treat you based on how you treat yourself. When you hold yourself to a high standard, others will do the same. Act like the queen, expect nothing less, and watch people rise to the occasion.

My Notes: _____

_____

_____

34

MAKE APPOINTMENTS WITH YOURSELF

Inspired by:
Deya "Direct" Smith, Author

Set aside time in your schedule to take care of yourself. Treat yourself to a solo date, attend a yoga class, or spend some quiet time reading your favorite book. Whether it's an hour or 24 hours, you deserve downtime.

My Notes: _____

_____

_____

35

FALL IN LOVE WITH YOUR LIFE

Inspired by:
Charreah Jackson,
ESSENCE Magazine

"A woman turned on by her life is irresistible to the world."

Be content with where you are right at this moment. Find something that brings you joy that doesn't require the company of someone else. When you're passionate about something, your life has more meaning.

BE
AUTHENTIC

When
you're truly
comfortable in
your own skin,
you allow the
world to love you as
you are and appreciate
your genuine spirit.

My Notes: _____

_____

_____

_____

_____

I am *always* in
the right place
at the right
time.

Live BV Free

I remember having a conversation with
different women who have been treated for
Bacterial Vaginosis (BV), a smelly vaginal
discharge that affects women. What is even
more disturbing about this common infection is
that doctors nor experts can ever tell you the
exact cause or cure for the unwanted recurring
discharge.

At one time in my young adult life, I suffered
the shame of multiple infections. No matter
what I did to treat the symptoms, nothing
worked. Full of embarrassment, I paid the
copay to go see a doctor to explain my
symptoms, only to walk away with a prescription for one of those messy over-the-counter
creams.

NATURAL/HOMEOPATHIC HEALTH & WELLNESS REMEDIES

The medicine would clear up the infection for about a week and then the ole' faithful BV would return. This was one of the most annoying parts of the whole treatment process. I kept wasting money on "cures" that didn't work prescribed by a doctor who had no real answers.

The strangest part of this health scare was that it didn't matter whether I was sexually active or not. I would do anything to fight off the infection. I stopped using tampons and even switched soaps. After hours of Google research, I read countless stories from other

" I read [about] women who shared the same concerns with BV..."

women who shared the same concerns with BV, and started taking bits and pieces from each success story to create my own.

Here's the magic formula that finally rid me of BV forever: *(Remember to consult a doctor before trying any new regimen.)*

Apple Cider Vinegar. *(I told you it's my miracle juice).* Take a shot of ACV in the morning or dilute it with water and sip on it throughout the day. It will help alkalize your body and balance your pH which means you are in a less acidic state. Trust me. Drink this every day and you'll start to notice the difference.

**NATURAL/HOMEOPATHIC
HEALTH & WELLNESS
REMEDIES**

Take a Probiotic daily. Probiotics are the "good bacteria" that help promote normal vaginal pH. The most effective ones must remain refrigerated (e.g. yogurt).

Eliminate white sugar. Truth is, I have a serious sugar craving, but sugar is the culprit for thousands of ailments and illnesses (BV being one). The bacteria that combines to form BV actually feeds on sugar. In fact, it makes it grow rapidly. Make a healthier choice and replace white sugar with organic honey, agave, or another sugar substitute.

Garlic. Garlic is nature's antibiotic and can be taken at the first sign of infection. You can use it as a suppository or take it orally.

"IF YOU'RE SCARED
TO `PLAY THE GAME`
YOU'RE NEVER
GONNA WIN."

- KOE

37

PURSUE
YOUR
PASSION

Most of the time your passion is connected to your purpose. You must actively pursue the things that excite you. Think about what makes you smile. What could you do everyday if you didn't get paid for it? What has always been your interest, but you never went after it?

Make Room for
YOUR THOUGHTS

_____

_____

_____

_____

_____

_____

_____

_____

_____

_____

_____

_____

_____

_____

_____

_____

_____

_____

38

GO ON A WORD DIET

Instead of watching your calorie intake, monitor your negative comments. Successful people speak great things into their lives because they expect only the best for themselves. They understand the power of their words and stay focused on positive thoughts rather than filling their minds and mouths with negativity. Spend the next seven days observing

GO ON A WORD DIET

your thoughts and pay close attention to your words. Be sure to only speak greatness into your life and immediately replace any negative thoughts with positive ones. Keep track of the difference it makes.

My Notes: _____

_____

_____

"NOTHING IS TOO GOOD TO BE TRUE; NOTHING IS TOO GOOD TO LAST WHEN YOU LOOK TO GOD FOR YOUR GOOD."

- KOE

39

SHOW YOURSELF SOME LOVE (DAILY)

Here are 10 ways to promote self-love:

1. Do what feels good, not what looks good.
2. Treat yourself to a spa day.
3. Count your blessings and cast your burdens.
4. Stop asking for co-signers. Your approval is all that you need.
5. Let go of unhealthy habits.

39 CONTINUED

SHOW YOUR SELF SOME LOVE (DAILY)

6. Stop speaking negatively about yourself.

7. Take compliments without a rebuttal.

8. Pursue your passion.

9. Set new goals.

10. Try something new.

TURN OFF THE TV

"Poor people have big TVs. Rich people have big libraries."
- Jim Rohn

One of the best ways to know that you are learning and growing each day is to read. Reading is the best way to become a lifelong learner. Learning new information and opening yourself up to new perspectives is a very effective way to guarantee yourself

TURN OFF THE TV

personal and professional success. After all, you're not a real BOSS unless all areas of your life are aligned mentally, physically, spiritually, financially, and professionally. Here are four entrepreneur favorites that are sure to inspire creativity, empower you to reach for the stars, and enhance your spirit.

TURN OFF
THE TV

**The Boss
Book List:**
Invest in your
intellect and
#ReadADamnBook.

**[MASTER THE MONEY
MINDSET]** *Think & Grow
Rich* by Napoleon Hill

If you have ever listened to
rapper Rick Ross' 2014 album,
Mastermind, it is filled with interludes
from this Napoleon Hill book. He is the
brilliant mind behind the "Mastermind

TURN OFF THE TV

Principle" (two or more minds working together in perfect harmony for a common objective). This Boss bible has been called the most important financial book ever written. Hill teaches about the relationship between money and the mind, sharing ways to enhance your ability to consciously create an intention to be successful and find financial freedom. The book outlines

40 CONTINUED

TURN OFF
THE TV

success
secrets
including
hundreds of
history's most
successful men,
from Andrew Carnegie
to Henry Ford. This is a
MUST-READ for anyone
who dares to dream big, and
grow rich at the same time.

My Notes: _____

_____

_____

LIFESTYLE LESSONS   12?

40

CONTINUED

TURN OFF THE TV

[PERFECT YOUR PEOPLE SKILLS] *The Four Agreements* by Don Miguel Ruiz

This is a MUST-READ for personal development. It is nearly impossible to be successful in business when your thoughts are not aligned with your intentions. In *The Four Agreements*, Don Miguel Ruiz shares four principles to create love and happiness in

TURN OFF THE TV

your life. He also shares an in-depth look at how we developed our personalities, prejudices, and beliefs based on what we experienced as children. This book will help you reveal your deficiencies and replace them with positive alternatives with four principles everyone can appreciate.

TURN OFF THE TV

[MAKE
YOUR
MONEY WERK
FOR YOU]
Rich Dad, Poor Dad
by Robert Kiyosaki

Referred to as the #1
personal finance book of all
time, *Rich Dad, Poor Dad* tells
the childhood story of money
principles learned from a rich father
and a poor father. Author Robert
Kiyosaki teaches money saving,
making, and investment principles that he

TURN OFF THE TV

learned from the failures and successes of his father and his best friend's father. This book will change your perception of money and intensify your desire to dream big and make your money *WERK* for you.

[GET YA MIND RIGHT]

The Traveler's Gift by Andy Andrews

TURN OFF
THE TV

The only fiction book to make The Boss Book list is *The Traveler's Gift* by Andy Andrews. Through colorful stories and exciting adventures, he shares valuable life lessons that will determine personal success and offer you a greater insight and appreciation of LIFE. From seeking wisdom to choosing happiness and being a person of action, you are guaranteed to take

TURN OFF THE TV

away a valuable lesson that will aid in your personal and professional success. Wealthy people enjoy learning new things every single day. More important, they consciously apply their newfound knowledge because knowing something without taking action means nothing. While it is important to take-in new information, be

TURN OFF
THE TV

sure to apply it with new actions and intentions. No time to read? Purchase the audio-book or invest in a Kindle (which has an awesome feature that will read the book aloud). Another great way to add excitement to education is with a group of friends. Start a local reading group or join an online book club and connect with women who can share in the learning experience.

Make Room for
YOUR THOUGHTS

_____

_____

_____

_____

_____

_____

_____

_____

_____

_____

_____

_____

_____

_____

_____

_____

_____

41

BAD CREDIT AIN'T BOSSY

Inspired by:
Arnita Johnson,
Certified Credit
Consultant

Many times we suffer blows to our credit score due to pure ignorance. We simply do not know that the decisions we make with our money today are hurting our chance for a secure financial future. When it comes to marriages, financial issues are among the top reasons for divorce. I definitely want to avoid having an awkward and embarrassing

BAD
CREDIT
AIN'T
BOSSY

Inspired by:
Amita Johnson,
Certified Credit
Consultant

conver-
sation with
a potential
husband about
my low credit
score and high debt.
It's time to be proactive
by becoming financially
fluent before you jump the
broom.

*Did you know that only 1% of
Americans have an 800+ credit
score? Calm down if you are nowhere
close. Arnita Johnson, an advocate for*

BAD
CREDIT
AIN'T
BOSSY

*Inspired by:
Arnita Johnson,
Certified Credit
Consultant*

consumer
credit
awareness,
says that a good
score ranges
between 640-700.

4 Steps to Credit Repair

1. *Order Your Credit Report*
You are entitled to one free
copy of your credit report from
three national credit bureaus each
year. It is important that you actually
know what is on your report to make

BAD
CREDIT
AIN'T
BOSSY

Inspired by:
Amita Johnson,
Certified Credit
Consultant

sure that your information is up-to-date and accurate. If you are like me and want to fix your credit, visit www.AnnualCredit-Report.com to order your credit report and get to *WERK*.

2. *Avoid being 30 Days Late*
It takes 12 months to redeem yourself from one payment that is 30 days late.

BAD
CREDIT
AIN'T
BOSSY

Inspired by:
Amita Johnson,
Certified Credit
Consultant

Three 30-day late payments can negatively affect your overall credit score just as much as a bankruptcy. Pay at least your minimum payment by its due date. If at all possible, pay a little more than the minimum amount.

3. *Credit Cards Count*
Credit cards have the largest impact on your credit score. A secured credit

BAD CREDIT AIN'T BOSSY

Inspired by:
Arnita Johnson,
Certified Credit
Consultant

card
uses your
funds as
opposed to
lending funds with
interest. Please
note: These (revolving)
accounts do not ever
close on their own. You or
the lender must choose to
close it.

4. *Never Settle a Debt with a Collection Agency*
Unless they are able to prove that the

BAD
CREDIT
AIN'T
BOSSY

Inspired by:
Arnita Johnson,
Certified Credit
Consultant

debt is accurate and actually yours, refuse to settle. Many times third parties purchase your debt without the proper documentation needed to collect because uneducated and uninformed consumers often pay without requesting proper proof. Don't be a victim!

42

DON'T TAKE IT PERSONAL JUST BLAME THE RETRO GRADE

Whether you're into "astrology" or not, I'm almost certain you've felt the effects of Mercury's Retrograde. Retrograde is when the planet appears to be moving in reverse which causes different aspects of our lives to "move in reverse." Freaky stuff happens during retrograde: Two of my friends got into car wrecks, I found myself arguing a whole lot with

42 CONTINUED

DON'T TAKE IT PERSONAL JUST BLAME THE RETRO GRADE

my man, and a few of my business deals folded. This shift can cause technical difficulties, breakdown in communication, and it can make business dealing extremely difficult.

The only reason I managed to survive with my sanity is because I was ready. I had mentally prepared for the BS. You can't control your circum-

DON'T TAKE IT PERSONAL JUST BLAME THE RETRO GRADE

stances; you can only control your response to them. So, when mercury starts wreaking havoc, how will you handle it? Technical difficulties with your phone, computer, car, or relationships? **Don't take it personal, just blame the retrograde.** Good luck and may the force be with you.

43

"HOW YOU GONNA WIN WHEN YOU AIN'T RIGHT WITHIN?"

Lauryn Hill, Doo Wop (That Thing)

When you're completely comfortable and confident with who you are, there is no enemy that can defeat you. The one trait all winners must have is a positive mindset.

You get right within by believing in yourself, having faith in your superpowers, and not letting anyone stagger your success.

44

DARE TO DREAM (DREAM DAY)

Believing
is seeing. In
other words, if
you want to
convince yourself
that your dreams can
still come true, you'll
have an easier time
manifesting your desires if
you first visualize the possibilities (before they exist).

My Notes: _____

_____

_____

45

WHO'S IN YOUR CIRCLE?

Birds of a feather flock together. You represent the five people you are closest to. When you are constantly making changes for the better, your circle will begin to change. You will notice your mindset shifting and your thoughts becoming more conscious. Make an effort to surround yourself with people who will hold you accountable for being great.

WHO'S IN YOUR CIRCLE?

You are your friends. They are not simply a reflection of you. The people you share your world with show you how you feel about yourself and what you really want out of life. Take a moment to assess your circle of influence. If they aren't working with you, they're working against you, and their time is up. They do not deserve anymore of your energy.

46

GIVE UP WHAT IS WEIGHING YOU DOWN

Resilience. It is one of the most important life skills to develop. You have to be able to respond well to loss and disappointment and bounce right back. When you decide to improve your life, the first thing you begin to experience is loss. Pablo Picasso said, "Every act of creation is first of all an act of destruction." In other words, the wrong things

GIVE UP WHAT IS WEIGHING YOU DOWN

(bad relationships, self-sabotage) always fall apart before the right things (healthy bonds, great opportunities) come together. Make an effort to accept loss as part of the process and trust that an AMAZING new replacement is on its way.

I am an *irresistible* magnet to great and wonderful experiences.

Green Smoothies

Green smoothies are life-changing because they contain green leafy vegetables. Due to their high-content of antioxidants, these veggies may be one of the best cancer-preventing foods. Based on USDA reports, studies have shown that eating 2 to 3 servings of green leafy vegetables per week may lower the risk of stomach, breast, and skin cancer. These same antioxidants have also been proven to decrease the risk of heart disease.

" A green smoothie a day keeps the doctor away. "

NATURAL/HOMEOPATHIC HEALTH & WELLNESS REMEDIES

Here are five reasons to make green smoothies a part of your daily diet:

- Simple way to boost immune system
- Natural energy booster
- Packed with disease-fighting antioxidants
- Natural weight loss (when you include protein)
- The best fast food. You can make one in less than 10 minutes

For more info on green smoothies, visit:
www.simplegreensmoothies.com

THINK OUTSIDE THE PRESCRIPTION BOTTLE

47

GIRLS
COMPETE
QUEENS
COLLAB
ORATE

When
you are
operating in
your purpose,
there is no
competition. Nobody
can *WERK* your divine
plan like you. It was
created just for you. Don't
get caught up in competing
with anyone for anything
because what is meant for you is
already yours.

48

BE A BLESSING

The only way to guarantee continuous blessings is to be a blessing to others. Serve those in need whenever possible, in whatever way possible. When you are blessed, it is your duty to pay-it-forward.

My Notes: _____

_____

_____

49

GET COMFORTABLE WITH BEING UNCOMFORTABLE

Think about your most recent personal dilemma. Instead of wondering why something is happening to you, recognize that it is happening *for* you. Although the roadblocks we face can be painful, they are really catalysts for creativity and change. The experiences that cause the biggest breakthroughs are typically the ones that cause the biggest break-

GET COMFORTABLE WITH BEING UNCOMFORTABLE

downs. Embrace the uncomfortable change, look forward to your transformed future, and go confidently in the direction of your dreams.

My Notes: _____

_____

_____

My endless good now comes to me in endless ways. Today will be an amazing day.

50

THERE'S NOTHING WRONG WITH BEING NEEDY

A need is something that is essential or extremely important. You should never feel bad for needing something from someone you are in a relationship with (including friendships and family relationships). The key is to find a healthy way to express that need to others so that it doesn't become a toxic dependence.

51

DON'T GET MAD, GET MOTIVATED

Turn your obstacles into opportunities by allowing your creative spirit to takeover. Instead of feeling helpless and disgruntled when I see others crediting from my *WERK*, I channel that energy into creating something new— something to keep them guessing. I've learned to use all of the ammunition around me (both good and bad) to inspire and fuel my success.

52

SPEAK WHAT YOU SEEK UNTIL YOU SEE WHAT YOU'VE SAID

Complaining is a choice. Just as you choose what to wear, you choose what to say. Your life experiences can make you better or bitter; the choice is yours.

My Notes: _____

_____

_____

53

MASTERMIND YOUR WAY TO A MILLION

Create a weekly, monthly, or bi-annual mastermind meeting with your Dream Team where you share your profitable ideas and brainstorm intensely to create a solid strategy for success with a group of like-minded people.

54

GET YA 'ISH TOGETHER

What do you have to offer? There's nothing worse than a woman who expects a man to bring everything to the table while she shows up starving and looking thirsty.

4 Steps to Getting Ya 'Ish Together:

1. *Get REAL.* Take some time to do a deep self-reflection. What are you doing

GET YA 'ISH TOGETHER

with your
life? I mean
really. How
are you spend-
ing your time? Our
habits shape our
lives because we are
what we consistently do.
2. *Be specific by choosing
ONE area to focus on.*
Don't try to become a new
person overnight.
3. *Create a plan and write it out.*
There's just something about seeing it
on paper that impresses it in your

54 CONTINUED

GET YA 'ISH TOGETHER

sub-conscious. What steps are going to take to achieve your goal? Your steps must be carefully calculated and followed. Start slow, remain steady, and you'll finish strong.

4. *Get to WERK*.

Start moving in the direction of your goal and don't ever stop. You can't get anywhere by standing still. As long as you are making consistent

GET YA 'ISH
TOGETHER

strides
(in the right
direction), you
are bound to
succeed. I've
found that as long as
you are working toward
something, you'll consistently see improvements in
all areas of your life. Once
you begin achieving goals, you
will set larger ones and begin
holding yourself accountable to the
little voice in your head. You will learn
to trust yourself and your instincts

54 CONTINUED

GET YA 'ISH TOGETHER

because you will begin to see yourself as being successful. Successful people focus their energy on a specific goal and practice patience, persistence, and positivity until they achieve it.

My Notes: _____

_____

_____

55

ARE YOU A DRAMA QUEEN, TRAUMA QUEEN OR BEAUTY QUEEN?

Inspired by:
Shaneka McClarty,
Licensed Therapist

What kind of Queen are you? Choose wisely.

- **Drama** *[drah-muh, dram-uh]* noun. always mad, hard to deal with
- **Trauma** *[trou-muh, traw-ma]* noun. hurt, guarded and emotionally damaged
- **Beauty** *[byoo-tee]* noun. constantly seeking improvement, growth, and happiness

I now release
everything that is not
divinely designed
for me and create
space for all that
I deserve.

You Are What You Eat

According to a study done by 9th Mind Media, ninety-three percent of the food we eat isn't even real. It has zero nutritional value and actually harms us more than it helps us. When it comes to your health, ignorance is not bliss. The only way we can nourish our bodies is by eating foods that are full of the nutrients we need. Dead foods are the chemical preservatives or food cooked with high heat that makes us sluggish, lethargic causing *"itis."* On the contrary, food is supposed to energize us and make us feel alive. In addition to how it makes us feel, the food we consume has also been linked to many of the illnesses and diseases we commonly suffer from. In my research to find the relationship between food and disease, I stumbled upon Alfredo Bowman, better known as Dr. Sebi, a pathologist, herbalist, biochemist, naturalist, and founder of the USHA Research Institute in Honduras. He's credited with over 28 years of using natural remedies to successfully cure diseases deemed "incurable" by modern medicine *(Dr. Sebi's definitely Google worthy)*.

In order to make the most of our mealtimes, it is important to pack each meal with electric foods. An electric food is one that is completely natural, of the Earth, and is alive. Here's a list of electric foods to grab during your next trip to the grocery store:

Fruit (no seedless or canned): Apples, bananas, berries, mangos, oranges, peaches, pears, plum, melons, grapes, and cantaloupe.

Nuts: Raw almonds and almond butter, raw sesame seeds, raw sesame, Tahini butter, walnuts, and hazelnut.

Grains: Amaranth, Kamut, quinoa, rye, spelt, teff, and wild rice (black).

Greens: Kale, turnip, dandelion mustard greens, lettuce (all except iceberg), nopales (Mexican cactus), poke salad, and spinach (use sparingly).

Teas: Alvaca, anise, chamomile cloves, fennel, ginger lemon grass, red raspberry, and sea moss tea.

56

PERCEPTION IS REALITY

Today, I challenge you to check yourself by finding out how others perceive you. Take an inventory of your character by trying this little experiment and see what type of responses you get. Send a text message to three people and ask, "What are three words you would use to describe me?"

"WITH EVERY RISING OF THE SUN, THINK OF LIFE AS JUST BEGUN. "

- UNKNOWN

57

WHO GON' CHECK YOU, BOO?

Take back your control. You are in control of your happiness and have every right to defend yourself (although it is not even worth it half the time). What we have to realize is that we are giving people the authority over us when we accept their criticism, negative opinions, or bad energy.

Figure out *your* feelings so others can't

WHO GON'T CHECK YOU, BOO?

put theirs
off on you.
People will
quickly realize
who they can and
can't push their
negative energy off on.
When they see that they
can't affect you, they'll stop
trying.

Don't be so quick to ask what they
think. All the answers you need
come from within. Learn to trust yourself more than you trust the opinions of

57 CONTINUED

WHO GON'
CHECK
YOU,
BOO?

others. Learn self-control. A lack of self-control will lead to your suffering. Remember, you are not in control of circumstances, but you can control your reaction to them.

My Notes: _____

_____

_____

_____

_____

_____

_____

_____

_____

_____

_____

_____

_____

_____

_____

_____

_____

_____

58

AVOID
NEGATIVE
NANCY

Misery loves company, and negative people love negativity. They won't be happy until you're unhappy, too. You know they're coming, so don't be surprised. Be ready and move out the way.

My Notes: _____

_____

_____

···· I AM OPEN ····
TO RECEIVE
ALL THAT GOD
HAS FOR ME.

59

YOU GET WHAT YOU GIVE

Karma is real! When you give good, you get good. Go out of your way to be good to someone today, and watch how quickly the favor is returned.

My Notes: _____

_____

_____

60

KNOW YOUR LIMITS

There are None.

"FEAR KNOCKED AT THE DOOR BUT WHEN FAITH ANSWERED NO ONE WAS HOME."

- ENGLISH PROVERB

COMPLIMENTS ARE CRUCIAL

Be flattering. Flirt with people everywhere you go by giving them genuine compliments. It is possible to find something you like about everyone. It's such an easy way to instantly brighten their day.

My Notes: _____

_____

_____

62

DARE
TO BE
BARE

Be transparent. Every once in awhile, go without makeup. You would be surprised by how many men actually prefer a natural look. When you're dating someone new, try showing up with no makeup *(I wouldn't recommend this on the first date because first impressions last forever)*. But after you break-the-ice, be bold by showing him you're

DARE
TO BE
BARE

comfort-
able in his
presence and
confident in
yourself.

My Notes: _____

_____

_____

_____

_____

_____

63

WEALTHY PEOPLE DON'T WORK FOR PEOPLE

"If you don't follow your dreams, you'll end up working for someone who followed theirs." I understand that everyone does not aspire to become an entrepreneur. But I also realize that our generation has been trained to believe in the work system instead of being properly educated about the wealth system. Real wealth takes *WERK*.

WEALTHY
PEOPLE DON'T
WORK FOR
PEOPLE

It takes time, dedication, effort, and energy to build a business into a successful company. But the same formula is very similar, if not equal to the work you are already putting into building someone else's business.

Still on the fence about whether you deserve to design your destiny and live a life that you love?

63 CONTINUED

WEALTHY
PEOPLE DON'T
WORK FOR
PEOPLE

Here are
five
reasons to
Be your own
boss (BYOB)

**1. The essence of life
is in pursuing your
purpose.**

You may be a natural at your
job, and you may even enjoy
your work, but that doesn't mean
you are pursuing your passion.
You're only given a chance at living
this life one time. Knowing this, why

WEALTHY
PEOPLE DON'T
WORK FOR
PEOPLE

waste it
wandering
around aim-
lessly because
you're stuck in the
"cycle" or rat race of
life: Work, home,
sleep. Work, home,
sleep.

**2. You owe it to yourself to
follow your dreams and live life
to the fullest with no regrets.**
You deserve to see the fruits of your
labor. There is nothing more disappoint-

WEALTHY
PEOPLE DON'T
WORK FOR
PEOPLE

ing about working a corporate job for years and not seeing the fruits of your labor. After you've worked your fingers to the bone, spent your lunch hour at your desk, and missed your daughter's recital or son's tennis match all because of deadlines at work, do you receive anything more than a paycheck? Do you ever really see the benefits of

WEALTHY PEOPLE DON'T WORK FOR PEOPLE

busting your butt? I think not. As an entrepreneur, you directly benefit from all of your work. When you spend extra time on a project, you are rewarded with a loyal client. When you complete extra work, you get extra pay. Being your own boss puts you in control.

3. You can control your calendar.
Imagine being able to schedule your own

WEALTHY
PEOPLE DON'T
WORK FOR
PEOPLE

meetings,
choose
which tasks
are of most
importance, and
free up your time for
the things you really
want to do. That is the
life you are afforded when
you take a leap of faith into
entrepreneurship. You may
have to spend several late nights
putting in *WERK*, but I guarantee it
will be a completely different experience when you are on your own time.

WEALTHY PEOPLE DON'T WORK FOR PEOPLE

4. Live outside the box.

As an employee, you're forced to fit into the "corporate culture" and your personal freedoms are limited. You must dress within company standards, hide your personal imperfections for fear of termination, and behave the way they see fit so that you're properly representing their brand. Why not dictate your own life?

63 CONTINUED

WEALTHY
PEOPLE DON'T WORK FOR PEOPLE

You owe it to yourself to find your way out of the corporate box and elevate yourself to freedom. If you decide that you're finally brave enough to get that tattoo you've been wanting, you can make the appointment without fearing repercussions at work. Ready to try a new hairstyle? Have you thought about adding a pop of color or a spiky look to show off your

63 CONTINUED

WEALTHY PEOPLE DON'T WORK FOR PEOPLE

personality? Then you should be able to do just that. As an entrepreneur, you are able to step outside of the norm and live by your own creative rules.

5. No salary cap.

How much money do you want to make? The one thing I despised about teaching was the fact that no matter how hard I worked, how much

63 CONTINUED

WEALTHY
PEOPLE DON'T
WORK FOR
PEOPLE

overtime I spent with my kids, or how well they performed academically, my paycheck stayed the same. I could've been crowned Teacher of the Year and received praises for my students scoring the highest on the state-mandated test, or the worst performing educator in my building with failing students. It didn't matter. My low salary was set. Not long

WEALTHY PEOPLE DON'T WORK FOR PEOPLE

after this
did I realize
that the work
system wasn't
for me. And it is
only a matter of time
before hardworking
and dedicated employees
across the country under-
stand how much more
successful and profitable they
could be if they got creative with
their talents.

(See Lifestyle Lesson 6, Turn Your Pain into a Paycheck)

_____

_____

_____

_____

_____

_____

_____

_____

_____

_____

_____

_____

_____

_____

_____

_____

_____

64

ENTHUSIASM IS EVERY-THING

When you're excited about life, life greets you with excitement. Be optimistic about everything. Greet people and situations you face with joy, and you'll be amazed by how you are greeted in return.

My Notes: _____

_____

_____

65

INVEST IN
YOURSELF

Be very
strategic
with how you
treat yourself.
What are you
putting in and on
your body? What are
you listening to? A
dollar-menu diet yields a
dollar-menu mindset.

My Notes: _____

_____

_____

66

EVALUATE YOUR VALUES

Most of our ideas, beliefs, and values have been passed down from our parents. We unconsciously follow their lead (sometimes for our entire lives) without questioning WHY we believe what we believe.

My Notes: _____

_____

_____

"ALWAYS BE READY TO HAVE THE TIME OF YOUR LIFE."

- UNKNOWN

67

DEDICATE A DAY

Choose a day to set aside and spend with your friends and family. These are the people who love and support you. Remain connected to them without ruining your tight schedule.

My Notes: _____

_____

_____

Make Room for
YOUR THOUGHTS

_____

_____

_____

_____

_____

_____

_____

_____

_____

_____

_____

_____

_____

_____

_____

_____

_____

67

DEDICATE A DAY

Choose a day to set aside and spend with your friends and family. These are the people who love and support you. Remain connected to them without ruining your tight schedule.

My Notes: _____

_____

_____

Miracles & blessings
are making their way
to me right now.

TAKE THE KOEK BOTTLE CHALLENGE

I took a personal health challenge and lost more than 20 pounds and dropped three dress sizes all from eliminating meat from my diet. But I still didn't have the shape I wanted. Since I'm super small up top with pretty wide hips, my ideal shape was the 'Coke Bottle' figure. My body literally remained the exact same shape, just smaller.

68 CONTINUED

TAKE THE
KOEK BOTTLE
CHALLENGE

I couldn't believe I had lost so much weight, but still had a bad case of the muffin-top syndrome. In addition to losing my love handles, I also wanted to lift my butt. Going from weighing 155 to 135 pounds meant losing my butt. It was as if it completely fell off. Although I liked being called "skinny," I really missed being called, "thick." It was then that I

68

TAKE THE
KOEK BOTTLE
CHALLENGE

realized I had to be strategic and specifically target the areas I wanted to improve. So, I came up with a plan to get my ideal figure.

Step One: Eat veggies daily

When I was introduced to electric foods (energy providing foods that are all-natural and 100% living), I completely changed my diet. I'm not a

68 CONTINUED

TAKE THE
KOEK BOTTLE
CHALLENGE

vegan or even a vegetarian because I still eat seafood. But, I eat mostly vegetables. My favorites are spinach, green beans, cabbage, and mushrooms. There's so many ways you can prepare a healthy veggie meal. I like to make a loaded veggie potato, add them as a side with rice or whole wheat pasta, or with shrimp or fish. I find creative ways to

TAKE THE
KOEK BOTTLE
CHALLENGE

make
them
delicious, and
it's so worth it.

Step Two: Squats
no shots

One thing I KNOW is that
if you do no SQUATS you
will have no butt. No matter
how much they hurt or how bad
you hate doing them, they really
work. Here's a bonus: Squats also
tone your overall body, not just your
butt.

68 CONTINUED

TAKE THE
KOEK BOTTLE
CHALLENGE

Step Three: Apple Cider Vinegar (ACV)

Did I mention that there are tremendous health benefits with this miracle juice? Of course, I did. And weight loss is no exception to this magical potion. By stabilizing blood sugar for a longer period, ACV helps cut cravings and controls the appetite. However, if your diet sucks, don't think a few teaspoons is

TAKE THE
KOEK BOTTLE
CHALLENGE

gonna do
the trick.
You may need
to revisit Step
#1.

Step Four: *WERK*out

Find a fun way to
workout the specific areas
of need. Search www.Grou-
pon.com to try out different
dance studios or fitness trainers.
You can even find a variety of
amazing at-home workouts on
www.YouTube.com.

TAKE THE
KOEK BOTTLE
CHALLENGE

Step Five: Waist train

Say what you may, but I experienced great results using my waist trainer daily. Since my goal was to cinch my mid-area, this hourglass shaper was a good investment.

Disclaimer: Be sure to do your research before trying any new weight loss tricks.

CREATE A
WERK
SPACE

Make
your office
a sacred
space to create
magic. Here are
five MUST-HAVEs:

1. An inspiration wall
An inspiration wall serves
as a constant reminder of
what you're working toward. No
matter where you glance, your
eyes land on words that make you
feel good. Words like "Fearless,"
"Faith," "Imagine," and all things bright,

CREATE A
WERK
SPACE

colorful, and bold (just like me) are what you'll find in my *WERK*-space. You can include goals that you've set for yourself, positive affirmations, prosperity post-it notes, success catch-phrases, a vision board and any other source of inspiration that can keep you cool, calm, collected, and connected when the pressures of your workday arises.

69 CONTINUED

CREATE A
WERK
SPACE

2. An idea note-book

My mentor once said, *"God is not required to repeat Himself. When He gives you inspiration, it is up to you to make the most of it."* I've spent years telling myself, I'll write it down later and let several great ideas slip away from me. These days, I will jot down an idea on any random piece of paper I can find, just to get it out of my

69 CONTINUED

CREATE A
WERK
SPACE

head. In my office, I keep a sacred million-dollar idea notebook. This one is specifically for the grand ideas I come up with that I will one day execute with ease. Invest in a notebook or journal that has an inspirational quote, a catchy phrase, or a neat design. Keep it with you wherever you go, so whenever you get a thought you can write it down.

CREATE A
WERK
SPACE

3. Reading material

Discover new things in a book. When you find yourself experiencing writer's block or letting your workload weigh you down, books are a great source of motivation. Some of my favorite titles that I can always count on when I'm in need of motivation and a quick reality check are *The Psychology of Winning* by Dennis Waitley and *The Game of Life*

CREATE A
WERK
SPACE

by
Florence
Scovel Shinn.
Find a few that
are meaningful to
you and keep them
on your office book-
shelf.

4. Apple MacBook

Once upon a time, I was a
diehard PC lover (before I become
an entrepreneur). Over the years,
my Macbook has been one of the best
investments I've made. Applications like

CREATE A
WERK
SPACE

iPhoto, Garage-Band, and iMovie are ideal for any small business owner who deals with technology ... and that would be ALL of us.

5. Wireless printer

Most often, entrepreneurs operate from their laptops and smartphones. If this is the case, having a wireless printer is less hassle and less time-

CREATE A
WERK
SPACE

consuming than a traditional wired printer. The other feature with wireless printers is you can connect multiple devices to it fairly easily and as you know, our goal is to *WERK* smarter and not harder.

My Notes: _____

_____

_____

YOUR REQUEST DETERMINES YOUR ROUTE

Starting route. We have all made the mistake of leaving off the NW or SW portion of an address and ending up at a completely different destination. The universe works just like a navigation system. The more accurate you are with the destination you input, the closer it will take you to it. If you can get clear about your goals, you will be able to get there much quicker

70 CONTINUED

YOUR REQUEST DETERMINES YOUR ROUTE

and on a much easier route. When you're unclear about where you're going, it is going to be very hard for God to send you the roadmap.

My Notes: _____

_____

_____

220   LIFESTYLE LESSONS

YOU ARE WHAT YOU ATTRACT

Like attracts like and energy is everything. Dig deep to figure out what signals you've been sending out. Your mood, emotions, thoughts, intentions, actions, and words create the energy that you send out into the world and it is returned to the sender every single time. If you send out doubt, worry, and fear you are asking for more reasons to feel

YOU ARE
WHAT YOU
ATTRACT

doubt, worry, and fear. Likewise, if you release love, happiness, and faith, get ready to receive an abundance of all the joy your heart can hold.

My Notes: _____

_____

_____

YOU HAVE TO GET IN THE GAME TO WIN

Life is
NOT a
spectator
sport. Stop
sitting on the
sidelines cheering
on everyone else. Be
the star player in your life
and make big plays.

10 things winners do:

1.Winners take time for themselves
every single day.

YOU HAVE TO GET IN THE GAME TO WIN

2. Winners turn off the TV and invest in their intellect.

3. Winners look their best at all times, so they can feel good at all times.

4. Winners are great receivers.

5. Winners take blame and credit honestly and openly.

YOU HAVE TO GET IN THE GAME TO WIN

6. Winners invest in themselves.

7. Winners focus on the positive until they can improve the negative.

8. Winners create healthy habits.

9. Winners associate with other winners.

72 CONTINUED

YOU HAVE TO GET IN THE GAME TO WIN

10. Winners remain cool, calm, collected, and connected under pressure.

My Notes: _____

_____

_____

STRESS LESS.
SMILE MORE

According-
ing to the
American
Institute of
Stress, about
ninety percent of all
diseases, ailments,
and illnesses are consid-
ered stress related. So,
whether or not you realize
you're being affected by stress,
more than likely you are. There
are numerous stressors that may be
working your nerves, but the most
common ones are finances, bad relation-

STRESS LESS.
SMILE MORE

ships, and a bad job. In fact, I read somewhere that a bad job can be more stressful than unemployment. You owe it to yourself to do whatever it takes to stress less and smile more.

My Notes: _____

_____

_____

74

WERK.
PRAY.
SLAY.

Werk
Dedicate your life to your dreams

Pray
Ground yourself in faith

Slay
Show out in celebration of your success

75

NOTHING HAPPENS BY CHANCE

You are always in the right place at the right time (if you get your mind right). When you're in your lane following your heart and pursuing your God-given purpose, the doors will swing open, the opportunities will find you, and the fear will fade away. **YOU have something in you** that's begging to get out and once you figure out what it is, you're going to be unstoppable.

CONSIDER YOUR CORE

Who you are at your core has ALWAYS been the same. There were so many clues from my childhood that I would be an entrepreneur. I was literally obsessed with working. I spent the weekends and summers "assisting" my dad at his office and when I turned 14, I lied about my age and got hired at the local McDonald's. I've literally been

CONSIDER YOUR CORE

*WERK*ing ever since. From daycare centers to banks and pharmacies, I've worked in every single industry, exploring my interests. It is no surprise that I'm still exploring them as a serial entrepreneur.

My Notes: _____

_____

_____

Make Room for
YOUR THOUGHTS

_____

_____

_____

_____

_____

_____

_____

_____

_____

_____

_____

_____

_____

_____

_____

_____

_____

_____

77

YOU GET IT FROM YA MAMA

Whether you like it or not, you are probably a whole lot like your mother. If you're like most women, you've inherited her good and bad qualities. It wasn't until I read *Ms. Typed* by Dr. Michelle Callahan that I realized just how much I had picked up from my mom. Not only did I have her freckles, nose, and hips, but apparently I had her dating personality,

YOU GET IT
FROM YA
MAMA

too. While
reading this
book, I
realized that
what I saw in my
home as a little girl
had a great effect on
my adult life. The way my
mother handled stress
rubbed off on me. The way
she handled my dad rubbed off
on me   even her outlook on life
seemed to affect mine.

This new info caused a major "aha"

77
CONTINUED

YOU GET IT
FROM YA
MAMA

moment
for me so I
decided to dig
a little deeper
and analyze the
good and bad traits I
picked up from both of
my parents. I realized
why I never let a man "take
care of me." I learned how I
got to be so secretive and I
even learned where my inappro-
priate laugh came from *(Thanks
dad!)*. This newfound info shocked the
hell out of me and what you're about to

YOU GET IT FROM YA MAMA

to learn may surprise you, too!

My Notes: _____

_____

_____

_____

_____

it's time
TO PICK UP THE PIECES
DISCOVER
— YOUR —
Purpose
AND
GET-YOUR-LIFE-TOGETHER

 # WERK

CPSIA information can be obtained
at www.ICGtesting.com
Printed in the USA
LVOW01s2240191116

513759LV00001B/1/P